50 Premium Pizza Restaurant Dishes

By: Kelly Johnson

Table of Contents

- Truffle Mushroom Pizza
- Margherita Pizza with Buffalo Mozzarella
- Fig and Prosciutto Pizza
- Gourmet Four Cheese Pizza
- BBQ Chicken and Caramelized Onion Pizza
- Seafood Medley Pizza
- Spicy Italian Sausage and Peppers Pizza
- Prosciutto and Arugula Pizza
- Smoked Salmon and Cream Cheese Pizza
- Lobster and Garlic Butter Pizza
- White Pizza with Ricotta and Spinach
- Sicilian Style Pizza with Anchovies
- Fennel Sausage and Broccoli Rabe Pizza
- Truffle and Brie Pizza
- Pineapple and Jalapeño Pizza
- Roasted Vegetable and Goat Cheese Pizza
- Steak and Blue Cheese Pizza
- Chicken Alfredo Pizza
- Buffalo Chicken and Ranch Pizza
- Duck Confit and Caramelized Onion Pizza
- Caprese Pizza with Balsamic Reduction
- Pulled Pork and Pineapple Pizza
- Tuna and Red Onion Pizza
- Vegetarian Garden Supreme Pizza
- Shrimp Scampi Pizza
- Beef and Lamb Kofta Pizza
- Roast Beetroot and Ricotta Pizza
- Peking Duck Pizza
- Chorizo and Roasted Pepper Pizza
- Lamb and Feta Pizza
- Smoked Duck and Pomegranate Pizza
- Figs, Bacon, and Gorgonzola Pizza
- Gourmet Margarita Pizza with Pesto Drizzle
- Grilled Eggplant and Parmesan Pizza
- Pear, Walnuts, and Gorgonzola Pizza

- Prawns and Avocado Pizza
- Caviar and Creme Fraiche Pizza
- Ratatouille Pizza with Herb Sauce
- Sweet Potato and Sage Pizza
- Black Truffle and Fontina Cheese Pizza
- Crab and Corn Pizza
- Braised Short Rib and Caramelized Onion Pizza
- Mushroom and Thyme White Pizza
- Tandoori Chicken Pizza
- Egg and Bacon Breakfast Pizza
- Smoked Salmon and Capers Pizza
- Bacon, Apple, and Cheddar Pizza
- Pumpkin, Spinach, and Ricotta Pizza
- Salami and Olive Tapenade Pizza
- Lemon, Zucchini, and Ricotta Pizza

Truffle Mushroom Pizza

Ingredients:

- 1 pizza dough (store-bought or homemade)
- 1/2 cup truffle oil
- 1 1/2 cups mixed mushrooms (shiitake, cremini, and oyster)
- 1 cup shredded mozzarella cheese
- 1/4 cup grated parmesan cheese
- Fresh thyme leaves
- 1 tbsp olive oil
- Salt and pepper to taste

Instructions:

1. Preheat oven to 475°F (245°C).
2. Roll out the pizza dough and transfer it to a baking sheet or pizza stone.
3. In a pan, heat olive oil and sauté the mushrooms until soft and golden, about 5 minutes. Season with salt and pepper.
4. Drizzle a little truffle oil over the pizza dough, then layer with mozzarella cheese, sautéed mushrooms, and parmesan cheese.
5. Bake for 10-12 minutes or until the crust is golden.
6. After baking, drizzle with more truffle oil and garnish with fresh thyme.

Margherita Pizza with Buffalo Mozzarella

Ingredients:

- 1 pizza dough
- 1 cup pizza sauce
- 1 1/2 cups buffalo mozzarella cheese, torn
- Fresh basil leaves
- Olive oil
- Salt to taste

Instructions:

1. Preheat oven to 475°F (245°C).
2. Roll out the pizza dough and spread pizza sauce evenly on top.
3. Top with buffalo mozzarella, fresh basil leaves, and a pinch of salt.
4. Bake for 10-12 minutes, until the crust is crispy and the cheese is melted.
5. Drizzle with olive oil before serving.

Fig and Prosciutto Pizza

Ingredients:

- 1 pizza dough
- 1/4 cup olive oil
- 1/2 cup ricotta cheese
- 1/2 cup mozzarella cheese, shredded
- 4-5 fresh figs, sliced
- 4 oz prosciutto, thinly sliced
- Fresh arugula
- Balsamic glaze

Instructions:

1. Preheat oven to 475°F (245°C).
2. Roll out the pizza dough and brush with olive oil.
3. Spread ricotta cheese on the dough, then top with mozzarella cheese, fig slices, and prosciutto.
4. Bake for 10-12 minutes until the crust is golden.
5. Once out of the oven, top with fresh arugula and drizzle with balsamic glaze.

Gourmet Four Cheese Pizza

Ingredients:

- 1 pizza dough
- 1/2 cup tomato sauce
- 1/2 cup mozzarella cheese, shredded
- 1/2 cup gorgonzola cheese, crumbled
- 1/2 cup goat cheese, crumbled
- 1/2 cup parmesan cheese, grated
- Fresh basil leaves

Instructions:

1. Preheat oven to 475°F (245°C).
2. Roll out the pizza dough and spread tomato sauce evenly over the dough.
3. Sprinkle mozzarella, gorgonzola, goat cheese, and parmesan on top.
4. Bake for 10-12 minutes, until the cheese is melted and bubbly.
5. After baking, garnish with fresh basil leaves before serving.

BBQ Chicken and Caramelized Onion Pizza

Ingredients:

- 1 pizza dough
- 1/2 cup BBQ sauce
- 1 1/2 cups cooked chicken breast, shredded
- 1/2 cup caramelized onions
- 1/2 cup mozzarella cheese, shredded
- 1/2 cup cheddar cheese, shredded
- Fresh cilantro for garnish

Instructions:

1. Preheat oven to 475°F (245°C).
2. Roll out the pizza dough and spread BBQ sauce evenly.
3. Top with shredded chicken, caramelized onions, and both mozzarella and cheddar cheeses.
4. Bake for 10-12 minutes or until the crust is golden and the cheese is melted.
5. Garnish with fresh cilantro after baking.

Seafood Medley Pizza

Ingredients:

- 1 pizza dough
- 1/2 cup garlic butter sauce
- 1/2 cup mozzarella cheese, shredded
- 1/4 cup parmesan cheese, grated
- 1/2 cup cooked shrimp, chopped
- 1/2 cup scallops, cooked and sliced
- 1/2 cup mussels, cooked and shelled
- Fresh parsley for garnish

Instructions:

1. Preheat oven to 475°F (245°C).
2. Roll out the pizza dough and brush with garlic butter sauce.
3. Top with mozzarella, parmesan, and seafood medley (shrimp, scallops, and mussels).
4. Bake for 10-12 minutes, until the crust is golden and the cheese is bubbly.
5. Garnish with fresh parsley before serving.

Spicy Italian Sausage and Peppers Pizza

Ingredients:

- 1 pizza dough
- 1/2 cup pizza sauce
- 1 1/2 cups mozzarella cheese, shredded
- 2 spicy Italian sausages, cooked and crumbled
- 1 bell pepper, sliced
- 1 onion, sliced
- 1/4 tsp crushed red pepper flakes

Instructions:

1. Preheat oven to 475°F (245°C).
2. Roll out the pizza dough and spread pizza sauce evenly.
3. Top with mozzarella cheese, crumbled sausage, bell peppers, onions, and red pepper flakes.
4. Bake for 10-12 minutes or until the crust is golden and the cheese is melted.
5. Serve hot and enjoy!

Prosciutto and Arugula Pizza

Ingredients:

- 1 pizza dough
- 1/4 cup olive oil
- 1/2 cup mozzarella cheese, shredded
- 4 oz prosciutto, thinly sliced
- Fresh arugula
- Balsamic glaze

Instructions:

1. Preheat oven to 475°F (245°C).
2. Roll out the pizza dough and brush with olive oil.
3. Top with mozzarella cheese and bake for 8-10 minutes until the crust is golden and the cheese is melted.
4. Once out of the oven, layer with prosciutto and fresh arugula.
5. Drizzle with balsamic glaze before serving.

Smoked Salmon and Cream Cheese Pizza

Ingredients:

- 1 pizza dough
- 1/2 cup cream cheese, softened
- 1/2 cup sour cream
- 1 tbsp lemon juice
- 1 tsp dill
- 4 oz smoked salmon, thinly sliced
- Fresh dill for garnish

Instructions:

1. Preheat oven to 475°F (245°C).
2. Roll out the pizza dough and bake for 8-10 minutes until golden.
3. Mix cream cheese, sour cream, lemon juice, and dill. Spread this mixture on the baked crust.
4. Top with smoked salmon and garnish with fresh dill.
5. Serve immediately, garnished with extra lemon wedges if desired.

Lobster and Garlic Butter Pizza

Ingredients:

- 1 pizza dough
- 1/4 cup garlic butter sauce
- 1 cup cooked lobster meat, chopped
- 1/2 cup mozzarella cheese, shredded
- 1/4 cup parmesan cheese, grated
- 1/4 cup fresh parsley, chopped
- Lemon zest and juice (optional)

Instructions:

1. Preheat oven to 475°F (245°C).
2. Roll out the pizza dough and brush with garlic butter sauce.
3. Top with mozzarella, parmesan, and chopped lobster meat.
4. Bake for 10-12 minutes, until the crust is golden and the cheese is melted.
5. After baking, garnish with fresh parsley and a sprinkle of lemon zest and juice.

White Pizza with Ricotta and Spinach

Ingredients:

- 1 pizza dough
- 1/2 cup ricotta cheese
- 1/2 cup mozzarella cheese, shredded
- 1 cup fresh spinach, sautéed
- 1/4 cup parmesan cheese, grated
- 1 tbsp olive oil
- Salt and pepper to taste

Instructions:

1. Preheat oven to 475°F (245°C).
2. Roll out the pizza dough and spread ricotta cheese over the surface.
3. Top with sautéed spinach, mozzarella, and parmesan.
4. Drizzle with olive oil and season with salt and pepper.
5. Bake for 10-12 minutes, until the crust is golden and the cheese is bubbly.

Sicilian Style Pizza with Anchovies

Ingredients:

- 1 Sicilian-style pizza dough
- 1/2 cup pizza sauce
- 1 1/2 cups mozzarella cheese, shredded
- 6-8 anchovy fillets
- 1/2 red onion, thinly sliced
- Fresh oregano leaves

Instructions:

1. Preheat oven to 475°F (245°C).
2. Roll out the Sicilian-style pizza dough and spread pizza sauce on top.
3. Sprinkle mozzarella cheese evenly over the sauce.
4. Add anchovies, red onion, and fresh oregano.
5. Bake for 12-15 minutes or until the crust is crispy and the cheese is melted.

Fennel Sausage and Broccoli Rabe Pizza

Ingredients:

- 1 pizza dough
- 1/2 cup pizza sauce
- 1/2 cup mozzarella cheese, shredded
- 2 Italian fennel sausages, cooked and crumbled
- 1/2 cup broccoli rabe, sautéed
- 1/4 cup parmesan cheese, grated
- Red pepper flakes (optional)

Instructions:

1. Preheat oven to 475°F (245°C).
2. Roll out the pizza dough and spread pizza sauce over the surface.
3. Top with mozzarella cheese, crumbled fennel sausage, and sautéed broccoli rabe.
4. Sprinkle with parmesan cheese and red pepper flakes (optional).
5. Bake for 10-12 minutes, until the crust is golden and the cheese is melted.

Truffle and Brie Pizza

Ingredients:

- 1 pizza dough
- 1/4 cup truffle oil
- 1/2 cup brie cheese, sliced
- 1/2 cup mozzarella cheese, shredded
- Fresh thyme leaves
- Arugula for garnish

Instructions:

1. Preheat oven to 475°F (245°C).
2. Roll out the pizza dough and drizzle with truffle oil.
3. Layer with brie and mozzarella cheese.
4. Bake for 10-12 minutes, until the crust is golden and the cheese is melted.
5. Once baked, top with fresh thyme leaves and garnish with arugula.

Pineapple and Jalapeño Pizza

Ingredients:

- 1 pizza dough
- 1/2 cup pizza sauce
- 1 1/2 cups mozzarella cheese, shredded
- 1/2 cup pineapple chunks
- 1-2 fresh jalapeños, sliced
- 1/4 cup red onion, thinly sliced

Instructions:

1. Preheat oven to 475°F (245°C).
2. Roll out the pizza dough and spread pizza sauce over the surface.
3. Top with mozzarella cheese, pineapple chunks, jalapeño slices, and red onion.
4. Bake for 10-12 minutes, until the crust is golden and the cheese is melted.
5. Serve hot with an optional drizzle of chili oil.

Roasted Vegetable and Goat Cheese Pizza

Ingredients:

- 1 pizza dough
- 1/4 cup olive oil
- 1/2 cup goat cheese, crumbled
- 1/2 cup mozzarella cheese, shredded
- 1 cup mixed roasted vegetables (zucchini, bell peppers, eggplant)
- Fresh basil leaves

Instructions:

1. Preheat oven to 475°F (245°C).
2. Roll out the pizza dough and drizzle with olive oil.
3. Top with goat cheese, mozzarella, and roasted vegetables.
4. Bake for 10-12 minutes, until the crust is golden and the cheese is bubbly.
5. Garnish with fresh basil leaves before serving.

Steak and Blue Cheese Pizza

Ingredients:

- 1 pizza dough
- 1/2 cup pizza sauce
- 1 cup mozzarella cheese, shredded
- 1/2 cup blue cheese, crumbled
- 1/2 cup cooked steak, thinly sliced
- 1/4 cup caramelized onions
- Fresh arugula for garnish

Instructions:

1. Preheat oven to 475°F (245°C).
2. Roll out the pizza dough and spread pizza sauce evenly.
3. Top with mozzarella, blue cheese, steak slices, and caramelized onions.
4. Bake for 10-12 minutes, until the crust is golden and the cheese is melted.
5. After baking, top with fresh arugula.

Chicken Alfredo Pizza

Ingredients:

- 1 pizza dough
- 1/2 cup Alfredo sauce
- 1 1/2 cups cooked chicken breast, shredded
- 1/2 cup mozzarella cheese, shredded
- 1/4 cup parmesan cheese, grated
- Fresh parsley for garnish

Instructions:

1. Preheat oven to 475°F (245°C).
2. Roll out the pizza dough and spread Alfredo sauce evenly on top.
3. Top with shredded chicken, mozzarella, and parmesan cheese.
4. Bake for 10-12 minutes, until the crust is golden and the cheese is melted.
5. Garnish with fresh parsley before serving.

Buffalo Chicken and Ranch Pizza

Ingredients:

- 1 pizza dough
- 1/4 cup buffalo sauce
- 1 1/2 cups cooked chicken breast, shredded
- 1/2 cup mozzarella cheese, shredded
- 1/4 cup blue cheese, crumbled
- 2 tbsp ranch dressing
- Fresh cilantro for garnish

Instructions:

1. Preheat oven to 475°F (245°C).
2. Roll out the pizza dough and spread buffalo sauce over the surface.
3. Top with shredded chicken, mozzarella cheese, and blue cheese.
4. Bake for 10-12 minutes, until the crust is golden and the cheese is melted.
5. Drizzle with ranch dressing and garnish with fresh cilantro before serving.

Duck Confit and Caramelized Onion Pizza

Ingredients:

- 1 pizza dough
- 1/4 cup olive oil
- 1/2 cup mozzarella cheese, shredded
- 1/2 cup duck confit, shredded
- 1/2 cup caramelized onions
- Fresh thyme leaves
- 1/4 cup arugula for garnish
- Balsamic reduction for drizzle

Instructions:

1. Preheat oven to 475°F (245°C).
2. Roll out the pizza dough and drizzle with olive oil.
3. Top with mozzarella cheese, shredded duck confit, and caramelized onions.
4. Bake for 10-12 minutes, until the crust is golden and the cheese is melted.
5. Once baked, garnish with fresh thyme leaves and arugula.
6. Drizzle with balsamic reduction before serving.

Caprese Pizza with Balsamic Reduction

Ingredients:

- 1 pizza dough
- 1/4 cup olive oil
- 1/2 cup fresh mozzarella, torn into pieces
- 1 cup fresh tomatoes, sliced
- Fresh basil leaves
- Balsamic reduction for drizzle
- Salt and pepper to taste

Instructions:

1. Preheat oven to 475°F (245°C).
2. Roll out the pizza dough and brush with olive oil.
3. Top with fresh mozzarella, sliced tomatoes, and a few fresh basil leaves.
4. Bake for 10-12 minutes, until the crust is golden and the cheese is melted.
5. Once baked, drizzle with balsamic reduction and sprinkle with salt and pepper.

Pulled Pork and Pineapple Pizza

Ingredients:

- 1 pizza dough
- 1/2 cup barbecue sauce
- 1 1/2 cups pulled pork, cooked
- 1/2 cup pineapple chunks
- 1/2 cup mozzarella cheese, shredded
- 1/4 cup red onion, thinly sliced
- Fresh cilantro for garnish

Instructions:

1. Preheat oven to 475°F (245°C).
2. Roll out the pizza dough and spread barbecue sauce evenly over it.
3. Top with pulled pork, pineapple chunks, mozzarella cheese, and red onion.
4. Bake for 10-12 minutes, until the crust is golden and the cheese is melted.
5. Garnish with fresh cilantro before serving.

Tuna and Red Onion Pizza

Ingredients:

- 1 pizza dough
- 1/4 cup olive oil
- 1/2 cup mozzarella cheese, shredded
- 1 can tuna in oil, drained and flaked
- 1/2 red onion, thinly sliced
- 1 tbsp capers
- Fresh parsley for garnish
- Salt and pepper to taste

Instructions:

1. Preheat oven to 475°F (245°C).
2. Roll out the pizza dough and brush with olive oil.
3. Top with mozzarella cheese, flaked tuna, red onion, and capers.
4. Bake for 10-12 minutes, until the crust is golden and the cheese is melted.
5. Garnish with fresh parsley and season with salt and pepper before serving.

Vegetarian Garden Supreme Pizza

Ingredients:

- 1 pizza dough
- 1/2 cup pizza sauce
- 1 cup mozzarella cheese, shredded
- 1/2 cup bell peppers, sliced
- 1/2 cup zucchini, sliced
- 1/4 cup red onion, thinly sliced
- 1/4 cup olives, sliced
- 1/2 cup mushrooms, sliced
- Fresh basil leaves

Instructions:

1. Preheat oven to 475°F (245°C).
2. Roll out the pizza dough and spread pizza sauce evenly.
3. Top with mozzarella cheese and an assortment of vegetables (bell peppers, zucchini, red onion, olives, and mushrooms).
4. Bake for 10-12 minutes, until the crust is golden and the cheese is bubbly.
5. Garnish with fresh basil leaves before serving.

Shrimp Scampi Pizza

Ingredients:

- 1 pizza dough
- 1/4 cup garlic butter sauce
- 1/2 cup mozzarella cheese, shredded
- 1 lb shrimp, peeled and deveined
- 1/2 cup cherry tomatoes, halved
- 1/4 cup fresh parsley, chopped
- Lemon zest and juice (optional)

Instructions:

1. Preheat oven to 475°F (245°C).
2. Roll out the pizza dough and brush with garlic butter sauce.
3. Top with mozzarella cheese, shrimp, and cherry tomatoes.
4. Bake for 10-12 minutes, until the crust is golden and the shrimp are cooked through.
5. Garnish with fresh parsley and a squeeze of lemon juice before serving.

Beef and Lamb Kofta Pizza

Ingredients:

- 1 pizza dough
- 1/4 cup tzatziki sauce
- 1/2 cup mozzarella cheese, shredded
- 1/2 cup beef and lamb kofta, cooked and crumbled
- 1/4 red onion, thinly sliced
- Fresh parsley for garnish

Instructions:

1. Preheat oven to 475°F (245°C).
2. Roll out the pizza dough and spread tzatziki sauce evenly over it.
3. Top with mozzarella cheese, crumbled kofta, and red onion.
4. Bake for 10-12 minutes, until the crust is golden and the cheese is melted.
5. Garnish with fresh parsley before serving.

Roast Beetroot and Ricotta Pizza

Ingredients:

- 1 pizza dough
- 1/2 cup ricotta cheese
- 1/2 cup mozzarella cheese, shredded
- 1/2 cup roasted beetroot, sliced
- Fresh arugula for garnish
- Balsamic glaze for drizzle

Instructions:

1. Preheat oven to 475°F (245°C).
2. Roll out the pizza dough and spread ricotta cheese over it.
3. Top with mozzarella cheese and roasted beetroot slices.
4. Bake for 10-12 minutes, until the crust is golden and the cheese is melted.
5. Garnish with fresh arugula and drizzle with balsamic glaze before serving.

Peking Duck Pizza

Ingredients:

- 1 pizza dough
- 1/4 cup hoisin sauce
- 1/2 cup mozzarella cheese, shredded
- 1 cup cooked Peking duck, shredded
- 1/4 cup cucumber, thinly sliced
- Fresh cilantro for garnish

Instructions:

1. Preheat oven to 475°F (245°C).
2. Roll out the pizza dough and spread hoisin sauce over it.
3. Top with mozzarella cheese and shredded Peking duck.
4. Bake for 10-12 minutes, until the crust is golden and the cheese is melted.
5. Once baked, garnish with fresh cucumber slices and cilantro before serving.

Chorizo and Roasted Pepper Pizza

Ingredients:

- 1 pizza dough
- 1/2 cup pizza sauce
- 1/2 cup mozzarella cheese, shredded
- 1/2 cup chorizo, cooked and crumbled
- 1/2 cup roasted red pepper, sliced
- Fresh oregano for garnish

Instructions:

1. Preheat oven to 475°F (245°C).
2. Roll out the pizza dough and spread pizza sauce evenly.
3. Top with mozzarella cheese, crumbled chorizo, and roasted red peppers.
4. Bake for 10-12 minutes, until the crust is golden and the cheese is melted.
5. Garnish with fresh oregano before serving.

Lamb and Feta Pizza

Ingredients:

- 1 pizza dough
- 1/4 cup olive oil
- 1/2 cup mozzarella cheese, shredded
- 1/2 cup feta cheese, crumbled
- 1/2 cup cooked lamb, shredded
- Fresh mint leaves for garnish
- Lemon zest and juice (optional)

Instructions:

1. Preheat oven to 475°F (245°C).
2. Roll out the pizza dough and brush with olive oil.
3. Top with mozzarella cheese, crumbled feta, and shredded lamb.
4. Bake for 10-12 minutes, until the crust is golden and the cheese is melted.
5. Garnish with fresh mint leaves and a squeeze of lemon juice before serving.

Smoked Duck and Pomegranate Pizza

Ingredients:

- 1 pizza dough
- 1/4 cup olive oil
- 1/2 cup mozzarella cheese, shredded
- 1 cup smoked duck breast, thinly sliced
- 1/4 cup pomegranate seeds
- Fresh thyme leaves
- Balsamic reduction for drizzle

Instructions:

1. Preheat oven to 475°F (245°C).
2. Roll out the pizza dough and drizzle with olive oil.
3. Top with mozzarella cheese, smoked duck, and pomegranate seeds.
4. Bake for 10-12 minutes, until the crust is golden and the cheese is melted.
5. Garnish with fresh thyme leaves and drizzle with balsamic reduction before serving.

Figs, Bacon, and Gorgonzola Pizza

Ingredients:

- 1 pizza dough
- 1/4 cup olive oil
- 1/2 cup mozzarella cheese, shredded
- 1/4 cup gorgonzola cheese, crumbled
- 4-5 figs, sliced
- 4 slices bacon, cooked and crumbled
- Fresh arugula for garnish

Instructions:

1. Preheat oven to 475°F (245°C).
2. Roll out the pizza dough and brush with olive oil.
3. Top with mozzarella cheese, gorgonzola cheese, sliced figs, and crumbled bacon.
4. Bake for 10-12 minutes, until the crust is golden and the cheese is melted.
5. Garnish with fresh arugula before serving.

Gourmet Margherita Pizza with Pesto Drizzle

Ingredients:

- 1 pizza dough
- 1/2 cup pizza sauce
- 1/2 cup fresh mozzarella, torn into pieces
- 1/2 cup cherry tomatoes, halved
- Fresh basil leaves
- Pesto sauce for drizzle

Instructions:

1. Preheat oven to 475°F (245°C).
2. Roll out the pizza dough and spread pizza sauce evenly.
3. Top with fresh mozzarella, cherry tomatoes, and fresh basil leaves.
4. Bake for 10-12 minutes, until the crust is golden and the cheese is melted.
5. Drizzle with pesto sauce before serving.

Grilled Eggplant and Parmesan Pizza

Ingredients:

- 1 pizza dough
- 1/4 cup olive oil
- 1/2 cup mozzarella cheese, shredded
- 1 cup grilled eggplant, sliced
- 1/4 cup grated parmesan cheese
- Fresh basil leaves for garnish

Instructions:

1. Preheat oven to 475°F (245°C).
2. Roll out the pizza dough and drizzle with olive oil.
3. Top with mozzarella cheese, grilled eggplant, and parmesan cheese.
4. Bake for 10-12 minutes, until the crust is golden and the cheese is melted.
5. Garnish with fresh basil leaves before serving.

Pear, Walnuts, and Gorgonzola Pizza

Ingredients:

- 1 pizza dough
- 1/4 cup olive oil
- 1/2 cup mozzarella cheese, shredded
- 1/2 cup gorgonzola cheese, crumbled
- 1 pear, sliced thin
- 1/4 cup walnuts, chopped
- Fresh arugula for garnish

Instructions:

1. Preheat oven to 475°F (245°C).
2. Roll out the pizza dough and drizzle with olive oil.
3. Top with mozzarella cheese, gorgonzola cheese, pear slices, and walnuts.
4. Bake for 10-12 minutes, until the crust is golden and the cheese is melted.
5. Garnish with fresh arugula before serving.

Prawns and Avocado Pizza

Ingredients:

- 1 pizza dough
- 1/4 cup olive oil
- 1/2 cup mozzarella cheese, shredded
- 1 lb prawns, peeled and deveined
- 1 avocado, sliced
- Fresh cilantro for garnish
- Lime wedges for serving

Instructions:

1. Preheat oven to 475°F (245°C).
2. Roll out the pizza dough and brush with olive oil.
3. Top with mozzarella cheese and arrange prawns on the pizza.
4. Bake for 10-12 minutes, until the crust is golden and the prawns are cooked through.
5. Once baked, add fresh avocado slices and garnish with cilantro.
6. Serve with lime wedges on the side.

Caviar and Creme Fraiche Pizza

Ingredients:

- 1 pizza dough
- 1/4 cup olive oil
- 1/2 cup mozzarella cheese, shredded
- 2 tbsp crème fraîche
- 1/4 cup black caviar
- Fresh chives for garnish

Instructions:

1. Preheat oven to 475°F (245°C).
2. Roll out the pizza dough and brush with olive oil.
3. Top with mozzarella cheese and bake for 10-12 minutes, until the crust is golden and the cheese is melted.
4. Once baked, spread crème fraîche on top and garnish with caviar and fresh chives before serving.

Ratatouille Pizza with Herb Sauce

Ingredients:

- 1 pizza dough
- 1/4 cup olive oil
- 1/2 cup mozzarella cheese, shredded
- 1/2 cup ratatouille vegetables (zucchini, eggplant, bell peppers, tomatoes, and onions)
- Fresh thyme and basil leaves for garnish
- Herb sauce (parsley, garlic, olive oil, lemon juice)

Instructions:

1. Preheat oven to 475°F (245°C).
2. Roll out the pizza dough and drizzle with olive oil.
3. Top with mozzarella cheese and ratatouille vegetables.
4. Bake for 10-12 minutes, until the crust is golden and the cheese is melted.
5. Once baked, garnish with fresh thyme and basil leaves and drizzle with herb sauce before serving.

Sweet Potato and Sage Pizza

Ingredients:

- 1 pizza dough
- 1/4 cup olive oil
- 1/2 cup mozzarella cheese, shredded
- 1 small sweet potato, peeled and sliced thin
- 1/4 cup sage leaves, chopped
- 1/4 cup goat cheese, crumbled

Instructions:

1. Preheat oven to 475°F (245°C).
2. Roll out the pizza dough and drizzle with olive oil.
3. Top with mozzarella cheese, sweet potato slices, sage leaves, and crumbled goat cheese.
4. Bake for 10-12 minutes, until the crust is golden and the cheese is melted.
5. Serve with extra sage as garnish.

Black Truffle and Fontina Cheese Pizza

Ingredients:

- 1 pizza dough
- 1/4 cup olive oil
- 1/2 cup fontina cheese, shredded
- 1/4 cup black truffle, thinly sliced
- Fresh thyme leaves for garnish

Instructions:

1. Preheat oven to 475°F (245°C).
2. Roll out the pizza dough and drizzle with olive oil.
3. Top with fontina cheese and black truffle slices.
4. Bake for 10-12 minutes, until the crust is golden and the cheese is melted.
5. Garnish with fresh thyme leaves before serving.

Crab and Corn Pizza

Ingredients:

- 1 pizza dough
- 1/4 cup olive oil
- 1/2 cup mozzarella cheese, shredded
- 1/2 cup crab meat, cooked and shredded
- 1/4 cup corn kernels (fresh or frozen)
- Fresh parsley for garnish
- Lemon zest for garnish

Instructions:

1. Preheat oven to 475°F (245°C).
2. Roll out the pizza dough and brush with olive oil.
3. Top with mozzarella cheese, crab meat, and corn kernels.
4. Bake for 10-12 minutes, until the crust is golden and the cheese is melted.
5. Garnish with fresh parsley and lemon zest before serving.

Braised Short Rib and Caramelized Onion Pizza

Ingredients:

- 1 pizza dough
- 1/4 cup olive oil
- 1/2 cup mozzarella cheese, shredded
- 1/2 cup braised short ribs, shredded
- 1/4 cup caramelized onions
- Fresh rosemary for garnish

Instructions:

1. Preheat oven to 475°F (245°C).
2. Roll out the pizza dough and brush with olive oil.
3. Top with mozzarella cheese, braised short ribs, and caramelized onions.
4. Bake for 10-12 minutes, until the crust is golden and the cheese is melted.
5. Garnish with fresh rosemary before serving.

Mushroom and Thyme White Pizza

Ingredients:

- 1 pizza dough
- 1/4 cup olive oil
- 1/2 cup ricotta cheese
- 1/2 cup mozzarella cheese, shredded
- 1 cup mushrooms, sliced
- Fresh thyme leaves
- Garlic powder to taste

Instructions:

1. Preheat oven to 475°F (245°C).
2. Roll out the pizza dough and brush with olive oil.
3. Spread ricotta cheese evenly, then top with mozzarella cheese, sliced mushrooms, and fresh thyme leaves.
4. Sprinkle with garlic powder to taste.
5. Bake for 10-12 minutes, until the crust is golden and the cheese is melted.
6. Garnish with additional thyme before serving.

Tandoori Chicken Pizza

Ingredients:

- 1 pizza dough
- 1/4 cup olive oil
- 1/2 cup mozzarella cheese, shredded
- 1/2 cup tandoori chicken, cooked and sliced
- Red onion, thinly sliced
- Fresh cilantro for garnish
- Tandoori sauce for drizzle

Instructions:

1. Preheat oven to 475°F (245°C).
2. Roll out the pizza dough and brush with olive oil.
3. Top with mozzarella cheese, tandoori chicken, and red onion.
4. Bake for 10-12 minutes, until the crust is golden and the cheese is melted.
5. Drizzle with tandoori sauce and garnish with fresh cilantro before serving.

Egg and Bacon Breakfast Pizza

Ingredients:

- 1 pizza dough
- 1/4 cup olive oil
- 1/2 cup mozzarella cheese, shredded
- 4 slices bacon, cooked and crumbled
- 2 eggs
- Fresh chives for garnish

Instructions:

1. Preheat oven to 475°F (245°C).
2. Roll out the pizza dough and brush with olive oil.
3. Top with mozzarella cheese and crumbled bacon.
4. Create small wells on the pizza and crack the eggs into them.
5. Bake for 10-12 minutes, until the eggs are set and the crust is golden.
6. Garnish with fresh chives before serving.

Smoked Salmon and Capers Pizza

Ingredients:

- 1 pizza dough
- 1/4 cup olive oil
- 1/2 cup cream cheese, spreadable
- 1/2 cup smoked salmon, thinly sliced
- 1/4 cup capers
- Fresh dill for garnish
- Lemon wedges for serving

Instructions:

1. Preheat oven to 475°F (245°C).
2. Roll out the pizza dough and brush with olive oil.
3. Spread cream cheese evenly on the dough.
4. Top with smoked salmon and capers.
5. Bake for 8-10 minutes, until the crust is golden.
6. Garnish with fresh dill and serve with lemon wedges.

Bacon, Apple, and Cheddar Pizza

Ingredients:

- 1 pizza dough
- 1/4 cup olive oil
- 1/2 cup cheddar cheese, shredded
- 4 slices bacon, cooked and crumbled
- 1 apple, thinly sliced
- Fresh rosemary for garnish

Instructions:

1. Preheat oven to 475°F (245°C).
2. Roll out the pizza dough and brush with olive oil.
3. Top with cheddar cheese, crumbled bacon, and apple slices.
4. Bake for 10-12 minutes, until the crust is golden and the cheese is melted.
5. Garnish with fresh rosemary before serving.

Pumpkin, Spinach, and Ricotta Pizza

Ingredients:

- 1 pizza dough
- 1/4 cup olive oil
- 1/2 cup ricotta cheese
- 1/2 cup mozzarella cheese, shredded
- 1 cup pumpkin puree
- 1 cup spinach, wilted
- Fresh nutmeg for garnish

Instructions:

1. Preheat oven to 475°F (245°C).
2. Roll out the pizza dough and brush with olive oil.
3. Spread ricotta cheese on the dough, then top with mozzarella cheese, pumpkin puree, and spinach.
4. Bake for 10-12 minutes, until the crust is golden and the cheese is melted.
5. Garnish with a sprinkle of fresh nutmeg before serving.

Salami and Olive Tapenade Pizza

Ingredients:

- 1 pizza dough
- 1/4 cup olive oil
- 1/2 cup mozzarella cheese, shredded
- 1/2 cup salami, thinly sliced
- 1/4 cup olive tapenade
- Fresh basil for garnish

Instructions:

1. Preheat oven to 475°F (245°C).
2. Roll out the pizza dough and brush with olive oil.
3. Top with mozzarella cheese, salami slices, and olive tapenade.
4. Bake for 10-12 minutes, until the crust is golden and the cheese is melted.
5. Garnish with fresh basil before serving.

Lemon, Zucchini, and Ricotta Pizza

Ingredients:

- 1 pizza dough
- 1/4 cup olive oil
- 1/2 cup ricotta cheese
- 1/2 cup mozzarella cheese, shredded
- 1 zucchini, thinly sliced
- Lemon zest for garnish
- Fresh basil for garnish

Instructions:

1. Preheat oven to 475°F (245°C).
2. Roll out the pizza dough and brush with olive oil.
3. Spread ricotta cheese on the dough, then top with mozzarella cheese, zucchini slices, and lemon zest.
4. Bake for 10-12 minutes, until the crust is golden and the cheese is melted.
5. Garnish with fresh basil before serving.

www.ingramcontent.com/pod-product-compliance
Lightning Source LLC
LaVergne TN
LVHW061956070526
838199LV00060B/4149